The Flow

Journey to the Spirit of Surfing

BENTELI

by Dominik Baur & Biliana Roth

Flow describes the feeling of a blissful mental state of complete absorption in an activity that happens as if by itself.

– Unknown

Contents

Preface

During our journey we encounter people who tell us how they reach a state of flow during surfing and how this affects their lives.

The starting point for our road trip along the European Atlantic coast is a small community in northern France protected by towering cliffs. Yport is located on the English Channel in northern France around eight hours northwest of our home, in Switzerland. It is summer. Nevertheless, we put on sweaters and jackets as we eagerly head to the seashore. Small fishing boats rest on the pebble beach. Clouds come and go, allowing flashes of sunlight to peek forth then disappear again. We feel alternately hot and cold. We depend on nature, and as our journey unfolds, our connection to it grows. Beyond that, we have a feeling of freedom, of not being obliged to do anything, yet able to do anything. Across the nearly 11,000 kilometers from northern France to Spain, which our van called Alba handled excellently, the earth, sky, and water show a myriad different facets and sometimes it seems as if we are experiencing all four seasons in one single day. Every day, we look forward to opening a sort of "Black Box" – to find out who will we meet and what stories are waiting for us.

Normandy & Brittany

France

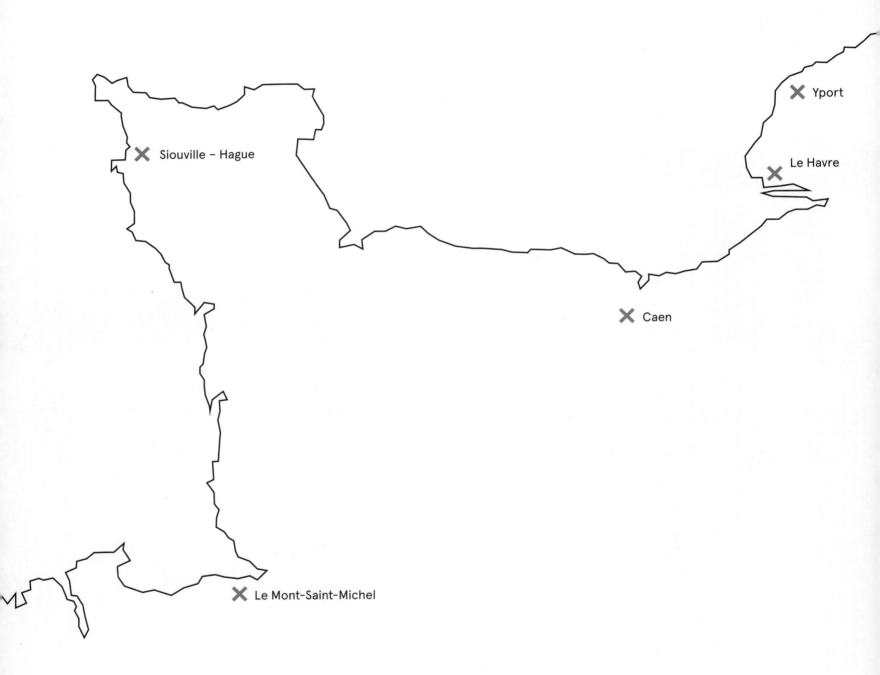

Yport

Le Havre

Siouville – Hague

Caen

Le Mont-Saint-Michel

Our days are fully dictated by nature.

On the first days, our path meanders through Normandy, the "Garden of France". Luscious green and gentle hills border the multifaceted coast of granite rocks and expansive sandy coves. We drive through romantic villages, past impressive half-timbered manor houses, and grazing cows. The gentle picture-book landscape with 4,000 hectares of protected natural habitats sets the mood for our adventure, despite the rather mediocre surfing conditions. The tidal forces are very strong, while the waves are usually too small.

Within a few days, we approach our actual destination in northwestern France – the Atlantic Ocean. In Brittany it presents itself in various colors ranging from silver gray to turquoise and navy blue, from calm and leaden to wild and raging. The 1,200-kilometer coast is interrupted by innumerable variably sized rocky and sandy coves, creating a special atmosphere.

Normandy & Brittany, France

Antoine

Surfing with my wife and my kids is the most precious thing in the world for me, there is nothing quite as relaxing.

THEN THERE IS THIS LIGHTNESS

Some people need the sea like the air that they breathe. This is why Antoine moved with his family to Morlaix, France. Spots are no more than 30 minutes drive away. Antoine makes money to support his family by trimming cow's hooves. It's freelance work which means there's always time to indulge his passion. The family man sets his work timetable according to the waves.

Antoine enjoys the feeling of being patient, of crossing boundaries, of being rewarded. "Then there is this lightness. Even though I weigh 90 kilograms, there is the sensation of being carried by the water, of gliding, accelerating, turning around, pulling up and down and taking off again, a feeling of simply having fun." However, it is the small things that fill him with happiness. "When at the end of a surf trip I simply jump over a wave, or once more see my son Glenn, who's been surfing the smaller waves near the shore, and I see how he's getting on. At such moments nothing else matters."

HIS BEST FRIEND – THE SEA

Antoine loves being close to nature. The sea became his best friend when he moved to Quimper, France in the 1990s at age 12. Back then he used to spend hours in the water, playing with the waves. Then something happened: "I used to swim in the waves until they rolled over me," Antoine says, remembering one particular lovely summer evening, "This time one of the waves didn't let go and took me with it. I glided in it, I was surfing."

At that time there weren't many people surfing, just the chosen few. "There was enough room for everyone. At the beach of La Torche you would see 50 to 60 people maximum in the water, today it is more like 200 or 300." More and more surfing schools and clubs opened, yet luckily there are still some secret spots, and surfing in winter. "Then we are about 10 people in the water and the conditions are simply fabulous," he enthuses.

I would lose my inner balance if I didn't hit the water today. I wouldn't be at peace with myself.

– Antoine

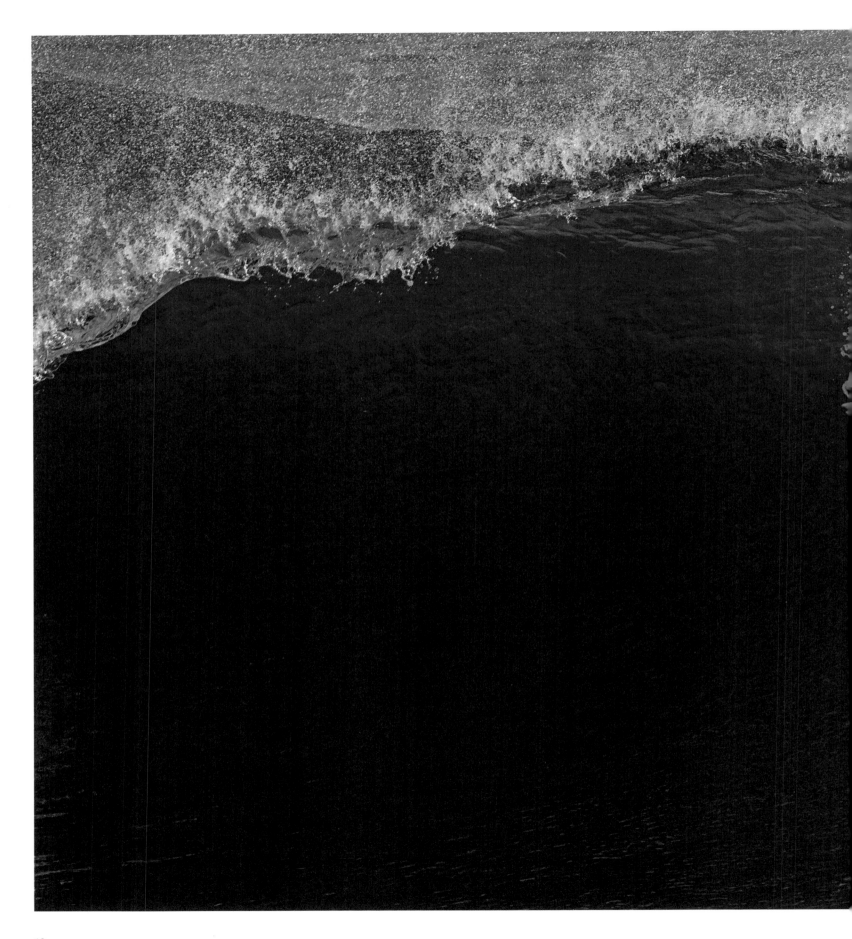

Normandy & Brittany, France

Eric

Eric was filled with an incredible feeling of happiness and deep pride when he surfed his first wave.

The lighting technician from Caen, France, experienced a profound healing effect at that particular moment: "When you are surfing, you forget everything. You exhaust yourself physically, which frees your head!" His first experience had such an effect on him, that he no longer even needs to be in the water to feel peace of mind. "When I feel bad and I can't get to sleep, I close my eyes and try to imagine being on a wave. In stress situations this is a true ZEN moment."

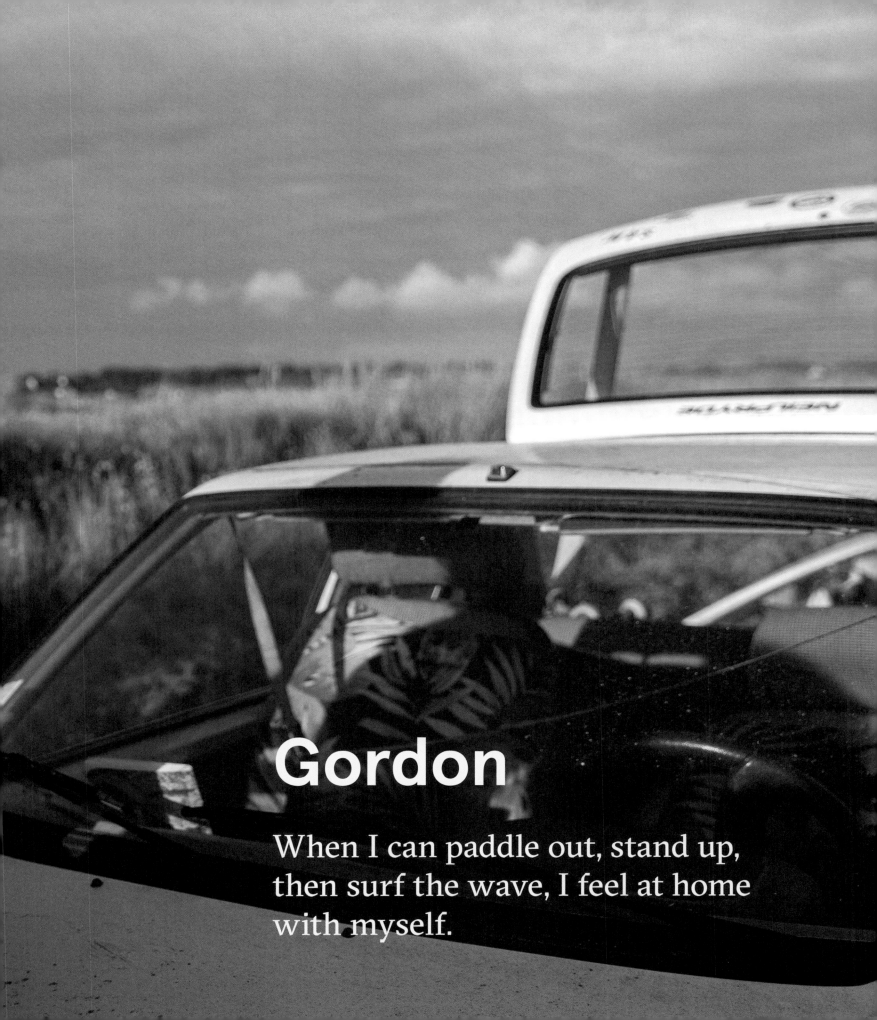

Gordon

When I can paddle out, stand up, then surf the wave, I feel at home with myself.

When you are riding the wave, on the one hand you're in control, and on the other you are in the flow. When you're in the flow you're tuned in. It just works.

– Gordon

Freedom rules Gordon's world. He has been living in La Torche for the past 10 years and he never stops surfing.

HIS MOTTO IN LIFE IS TO TAKE THINGS AS EASY AS POSSIBLE

Gordon smiles and explains that "out of the water" his ambition is to live a quiet life, keep out of trouble and not make waves. He spent the first 12 years of his life in Halle, East Germany. "Till the wall came down." That brutal border that split Germany in two, and locked up people like him inside their own country.

His trailer is parked on the 25-hectare plot of a local farmer, where 10 cows stroll about. Various other people have also settled here in trailers, huts, yurts, and campers. Gordon describes his home as "not a commune, but rather more of a small village." Friends also camp in this small community. His children, who live near Rennes, France, occasionally come to visit him. Whenever they're here, about an hour later lots and lots of young people turn up. They also find freedom here: "they live their lives as they please."

ARRIVING WHERE YOU FEEL AT HOME

In the summer, Gordon normally spends up to eight hours a day in the water. In the past few weeks an injury forced him to slow down. Today he was finally allowed

to set off again. With his surfboard on the roof of his car and a buddy. "When I parked my car, it basically felt like home!" He exclaims. When he heard that the waves were good, he immediately turned up the music, waxed his board, put on his wetsuit. He grins as if he were lapsing back into childhood, then Gordon sighs. When he is not surfing, things are very difficult. At such times he reads a lot of philosophy. However, he feels totally comfortable in water, because this is where he meets his family, all the people he knows. He is silent and then muses: "When I surf, I am close to myself and completely in my element."

GORDON SEES OBSTACLES AS AN ADVANTAGE

For example, when there are a lot of people in the water, "because you simply have to make an effort, cope with way things are at that particular moment. That's very easy for me," he stresses. He says he is not totally focused on the wave and always knows what is happening around him. That's why he is trying to teach his French friends the concept of "attentiveness", not being cautious, but rather being considerate of others, seamlessly fitting into the overall scene.

Normandy & Brittany, France

Soon after we pass the tourist magnet Le Mont-Saint-Michel, we find a steady swell and solitude, finally able to try our surfing luck. In Vauville we meet the quiet family man Antoine, who describes the sea as his best friend and so decided to move to this area. His expectations seem very modest. He's simply grateful for what he has. At the La Torche promontory, one of France's most famous surf spots, we meet Gordon who leads the kind of romantic nonconformist life that one would not expect to find in Europe. The gorgeous landscape of the Crozon peninsula offers enchanting contrasts of rough and gentle elements, while its picturesque villages of small stone houses invite visitors to linger longer. In Santec we experience an unforgettable example of the power of the weather. During a surf session with blue skies and sunshine, the weather suddenly turns. A torrential downpour interrupts our surf. The warm air is literally steaming and obscures our vision. Nevertheless, the sound of the rain drops as they beat on the sea gives us a very intense feeling of being happy to be in balance with nature.

Normandy & Brittany, France

Gironde & Les Landes

France

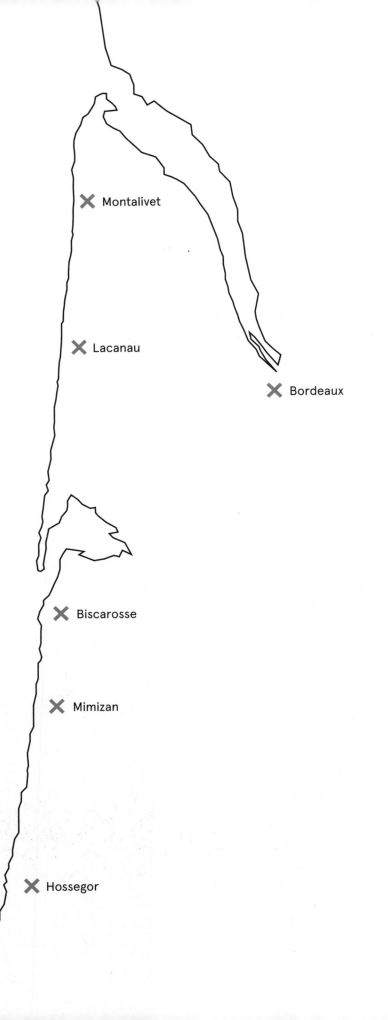

Montalivet

Lacanau

Bordeaux

Biscarosse

Mimizan

Hossegor

Pine forests and dunes border the shallow and open Atlantic coast of southwestern France. The Atlantic moves along this section of the coast without being interrupted by rock spurs and promontories.

On the way to the beach, sometimes driving down dead end roads, we breathe in the scent of pines and from a distance we can already glimpse the blue of the ocean and the white of the dunes between the slim trunks of the trees. Summer is still in the air. The rays of the sun warm us up as the wind cools us down. Is this already the perfect surfer life?

Together the Gironde and Les Landes regions have a 250-kilometer long coastline. Measuring 100 kilometers, the northern section is Europe's longest beach. Here, surfers of all skill levels can find the perfect wave. The changing currents and winds create expansive sand banks, sometimes within a few hours. This quickly changes the surf conditions. Nevertheless, you can always find suitable peaks, lovely rows of beach breaks, as well as whitewashes that roll ashore from far out and that allow long rides as well as worldclass barrels.

This is the reason why Gironde and Les Landes have evolved since the 1960s into a major attraction for surfers from all corners of the globe. Popular communities are Biscarosse, Capbreton, Contis, Hossegor, Mimizan, Moliets, Seignosse and many more.

In addition, a special lifestyle developed in the 1980s that dominates the scene to this day. There are camping sites, boutique hotels, or lodges everywhere, often directly on the beach. We actually stay at camping sites only every few days to wash our clothes and shower. They are usually so crowded that we are forced to look for alternatives. However, wild camping is illegal in France. Too bad that some people who do not abide by this rule litter the most beautiful locations.

If you just look around yourself, with a bit of luck you can find some simple camping areas, the Aires de Camping, some of which are located right on the beach. In such places, when you wake up in the morning you are greeted by your neighbor who is already wearing his wetsuit carrying his board as he crosses a springy cover of pine needles on his way to the water. The sound of the waves may be good or bad news, a look at the surfer forecast is more reliable. Today the waves are good in this location and somewhere else in the afternoon. We drive from one Aire de Camping to the next, discovering quiet and noisy places as well as interesting people. In Montalivet we spend the night at a camping site. We settle down for a few days here, surf daily, unpack the guitar and unwind.

Marco

On the wave, a void spreads inside you that brings you peace and joy.

IT AFFECTS MY VIEW OF THE ENVIRONMENT

Marco from Italy describes it as follows: "Your brain is simply entirely free and empty. It's like meditating. When your head is clear you get into a good mood and that is simply wonderful." Marco, a management consultant in the area of health and security, discovered that surfing helped him to relax. It also made him more environmentally aware. "I now feel much more respect towards nature."

IT WAS VERY TOUGH

Marco's passion for surfing began five years ago when friends told him about a trip to Cantabria, Spain. His curiosity was awakened and on the next trip he went with them. The first thing he learnt was that beginners must be very patient. The cold is a particular challenge for them. On a very cold day in February in Liguria, Italy, Marco ventured into the water when the air temperature was a mere 13 degrees. "It was very tough and was really no fun." He quit after an hour. He tried another time in April. This time he succeeded and surfing immediately became his great passion.

SOMETHING SPECIAL HAPPENED TO HIM

He felt very happy when he finally surfed his first wave. Something strange happened to him while he was in this flow, he can explain the experience, but not what happened to his mind. Just being able to remember the moment is all that matters to him.

When I look at the sea and see the pollution and all the bad things, that affects my view of the environment.

– Marco

Gironde & Les Landes, France

Elodie

Living in Bordeaux allows this university student to train as a teacher and also follow her passion of surfing and bodysurfing.

Bodysurfing is the possibly most natural form of surfing. Your body surfs on the unbroken wave, sometimes landing in it with the crest of the wave overhead. Elodie recalls a special moment. She was in the sea with some friends and the waves were a perfect two meters high. "It is impressive to see how quickly the wave closes and you find yourself in the middle of a barrel," she says excitedly.

In Capbreton, France, where Elodie spends every summer and has a job as a lifeguard, the waves often form barrels. "I am in love with the sea here," says Elodie. A life without waves – inconceivable. She realized that when she spent a year studying in Germany. She realized that the things she missed most were the beach and the sea.

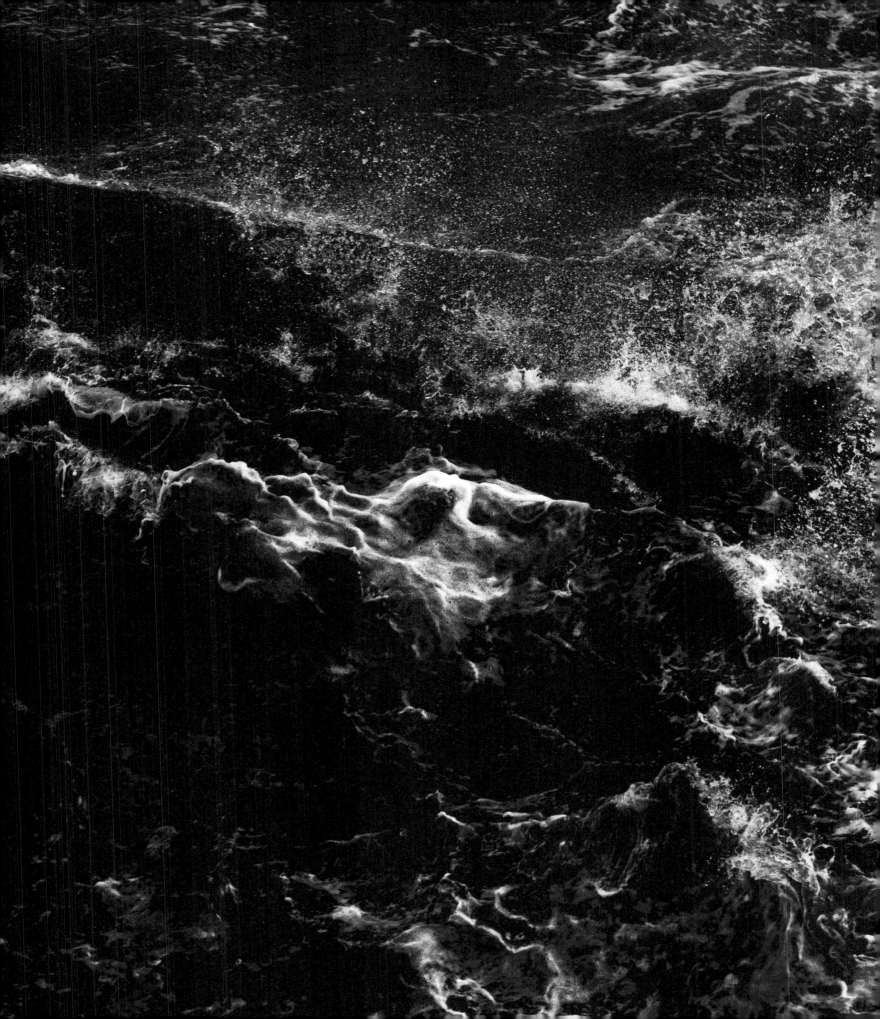

Gironde & Les Landes, France

Stephane

When I see the sunrise or walk along the small path to the sea – that is vital energy.

STEPHANE'S SECOND HOME IS IN MIMIZAN, FRANCE

The sports teacher from Toulouse, seems calm and satisfied with his life. The summers in the family's holiday home give him strength for the entire year. He doesn't need much to relax. Just reliving the same simple experiences is enough. When he's by the sea, he feels close to nature and his only concerns are questions like, "Will the wind be up tomorrow?"

LIVING THE MOMENT

Stephane reckons it's not about seeking thrills and excitement, "There is the satisfaction of overcoming your fear or just living the moment," he explains. "When I'm in the water early in the morning, just not having the ground under your feet, that's a special feeling,

that's good." Nevertheless, there's athlete's blood in Stephane's veins, "The adrenalin flows and you use this basic force to conquer and ride the wave." He starts to dream, "It's hard to put it into words. Man, your head, woooo! It all comes together, and it's time to do it all again."

VOILÀ, THIS IS IT!

Once, Stephane managed to surf 25 terrific waves in one go. There was no one else around because the waves were breaking far from the shore near a sunken ship. He said to himself "Voilà, this is it!" He reflects for a moment, "I feel great just going in the water. I don't even have to surf. I just love it all."

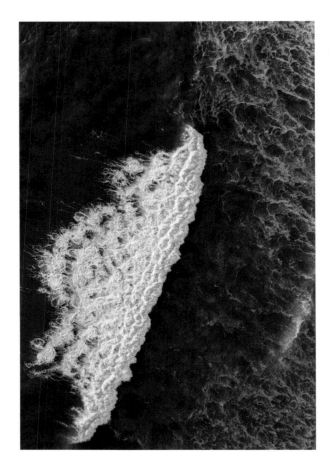

Gironde & Les Landes, France

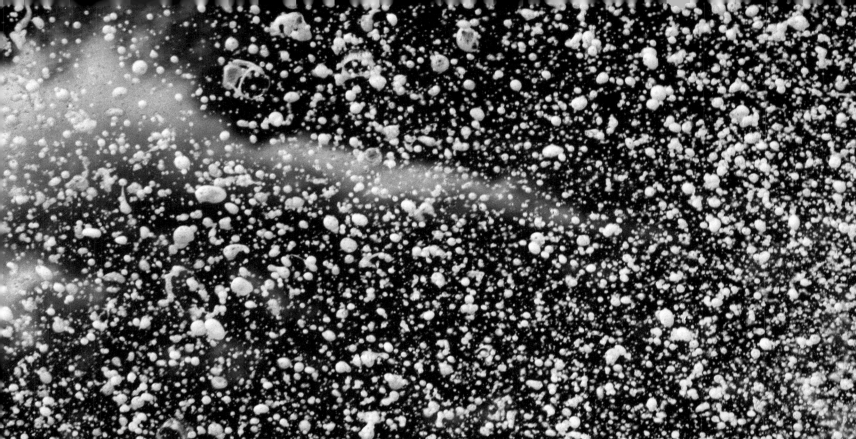

Colas & Axel

I enjoy being on the water with friends.
On the surfboard I feel relaxed and
experience a kind of complete satisfaction.

"Basically I just love surfing, I do try and get better at it,
but mainly I want to feel good and have fun. When I surf
a wave – the feeling is hard to describe. It is pure bliss.
It's ZEN – total peace. That relaxes me."

Being on the board is just incredibly cool. I love getting it right on the wave, playing with it and trying out new things.

– Axel

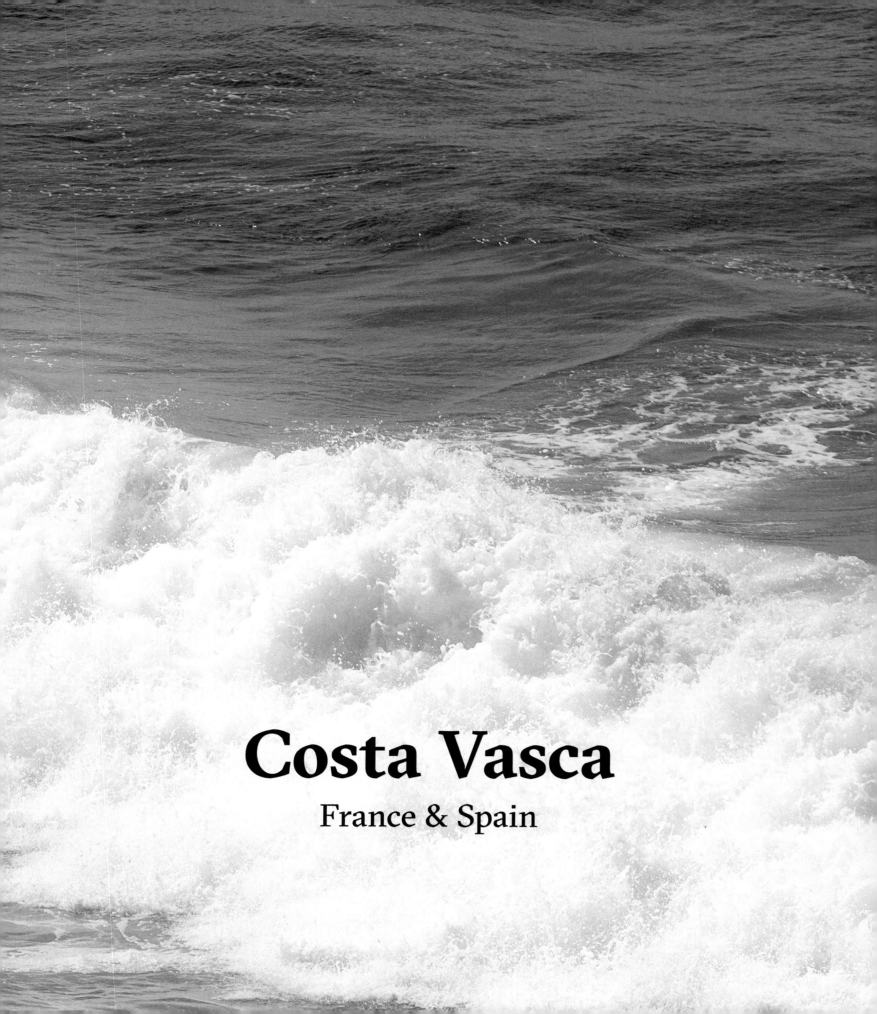

Costa Vasca

France & Spain

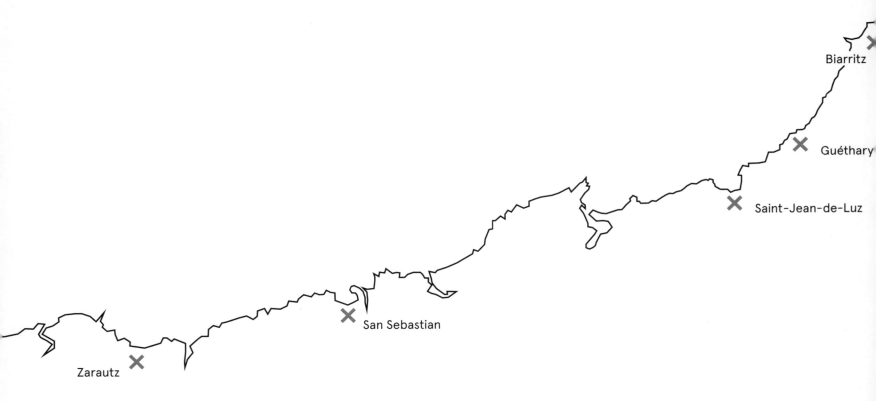

Biarritz

Guéthary

Saint-Jean-de-Luz

San Sebastian

Zarautz

The Pyrenees rise in the distance. Steep rocky coasts alternate with green hills. Coves of fine sand extend beneath them. Life is bustling, the beaches are full.

In Biarritz surfers carrying their boards past fancy boutiques. Surf instructors gather small groups on the Grand Plage, the large broad beach in front of the casino. Maybe it is too early in the year to follow the track of the flow here.

We make a short stay in Guéthary. It's the longboard hot spot, where the line up offers more room, but the waves are very tall and only suitable for experts, then after a visit to Saint-Jean-de-Luz , we drive to where the European continent takes a turn towards the west. This is where the Spanish Biskaya begins, a particularly stormy region. The Pyrenees are often covered in rainclouds. On the other side of the mountain range the landscape becomes more hilly again, the air remains humid. For our first night in Spanish Basque Country we drive along a panoramic road to San Sebastian, looking forward to surf sessions with a view of the city as well as to tasting the tapas of northern Spain, known as pintxos. We park Alba, our van, on a parking lot in the city center near La Concha, the shell-shaped beach with a regular swell. There are people in wetsuits, carrying boards. They brush the sand off in the middle of the city and use their buses as changing rooms. We spend the night here.

Lisa

Surfing is the hardest sport, the most difficult to learn.

YOU DON'T JUST DO IT FIVE TIMES AND THEN YOU'VE CRACKED IT

To surf you need to stay calm and not get frustrated. "Like today for example, everyone is asleep, you're the only one who gets up before 6am to surf. Then you check the conditions and realize oh no this is no good at all."

YOUR BODY IS SUFFUSED WITH ADRENALINE AND JOY

To succeed in daily life Lisa says you need patience, and the ability to fight. You also need to realize that in countries outside Europe people don't live in the same way. Surfing is similar to other sports. You have to step out of your comfort zone, and when you get it right your whole belly tenses up. Your body is suffused with adrenaline and joy. Everything else is a blank. But there's more to it than what happens in the flow. Even if it's all down to you when you're on the board, surfing is also about the other people you meet.

THE JOURNEYS, THE COUNTRIES AND THE PEOPLE

When she's traveling Lisa relies on her ability to make friends. She's ready to join in and have a good time. She wanted to extend her stay in El Salvador and needed to get a job. She just enquired among the other people in the water. It turned out that there was a man looking for a maths teacher for his Montessori school. It was like a dream come true says Lisa, "I got to know a lot of great dynamic people, could go surfing right before class, and then work with children which is something I love."

For Lisa El Salvador holds the memory of one of her most beautiful waves. It was a big one and she first needed to steel her nerves, but once she'd overcome her fear she was confident enough to go into the water. "The feeling of riding a large wave, of gliding along it and making the first turns, is just a feeling of great joy."

Surfing is a lot about the people you meet.

– Lisa

Costa Vasca, France & Spain

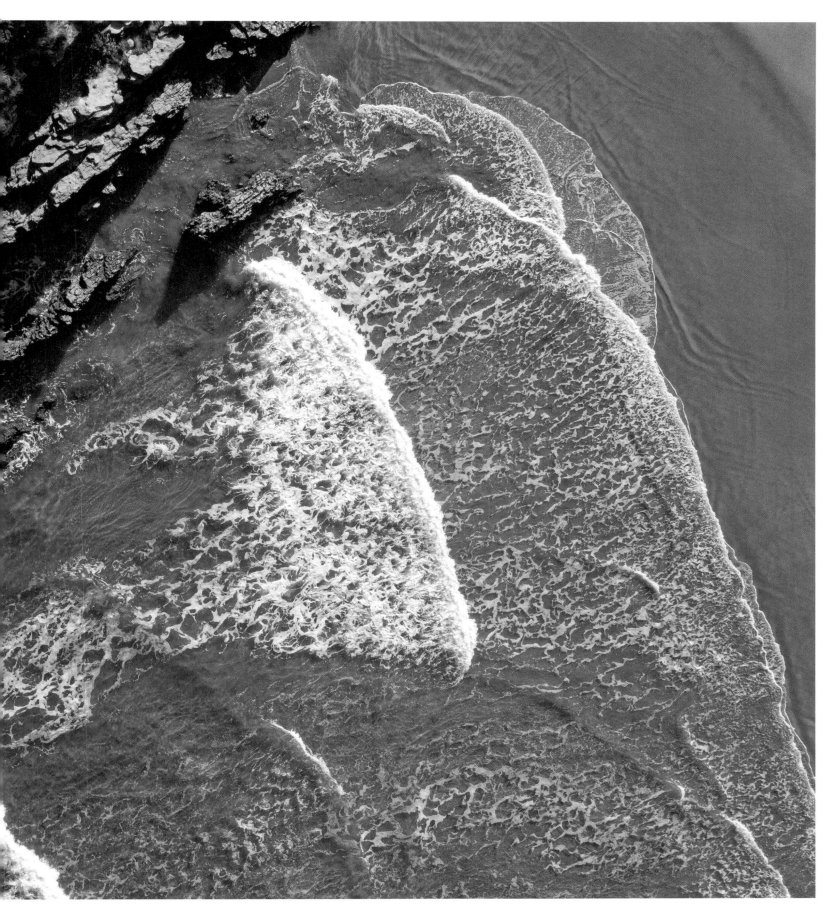

Costa Vasca, France & Spain

Fabrizio

Fabrizio works where other people come to spend their holidays. Four years ago, he became the captain of a 65-foot sailboat.

HE ENJOYS BEING ANCHORED IN A LOVELY COVE

It's a great job because he's always loved being near and in the water. The boat belongs to a family who only actually sail in summer or on the odd winter weekend. The captain, from Pisa, Italy doesn't mind sharing a small space with them and their friends. They get along fine, he says. "The best way to start the day is to jump into the water and go for a swim."

IT'S A LOT OF FUN

At the moment Fabrizio is on a roundtrip through Europe in his old van. The journey will take him from Switzerland, via Germany and France along the west coast towards southern Europe. "During the trip I've surfed almost everyday so I feel really tuned in to my board." He exhales powerfully. "It's all about fun. When a wave is very large it may make you feel very small, but it is still fun." What about when it get's too much? Things got risky in Guéthary, France once. That was a few years ago. He'd lost his longboard and suddenly there was a massive set. After the third wave he couldn't get out of the water on his own and his friends had to help him.

THE BEGINNING OF A TRUE LOVE STORY

Fabrizio doesn't need big words or thoughts to describe what he feels on the wave. He started off on a shortboard, but then one of friends got ill and lent him a longboard. It was at Les Cavaliers beach near Anglet. He was hooked. It was partly down to the board but also just the general atmosphere. "It was such a great place, I'll never forget the moment I fell in love with longboarding."

He says his wife Is cool about him having two loves in his life. In the months when he is at home with her in Italy he hardly does any surfing. The sea at home is as flat as a mirror for a whole month. "Ask my wife what I'm like then? I start to get very restless."

Along the coast towards Bilbao, there are numerous untouched spots and impressive views. We have a meal on the edge of a cliff, wash our laundry at the parking lot of a lighthouse, later climb down a cove to the water and spend the night with a view of the sea. While the unstable weather is a bit tiresome at times, there are fewer people and nature is more untamed.

Then we reach a place where the feeling of freedom is overwhelming. In Liendo we have the sea to ourselves. On its cliff-fringed beach there are only three other campers. In the morning there is a surprisingly loud knock on our van. The police wake us rather roughly, but only to tell us that we had left our camping equipment outside.

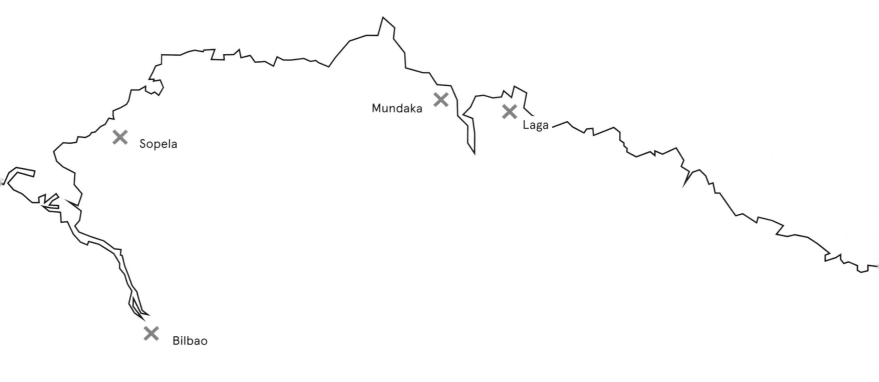

Mundaka

Laga

Sopela

Bilbao

Costa Vasca, France & Spain

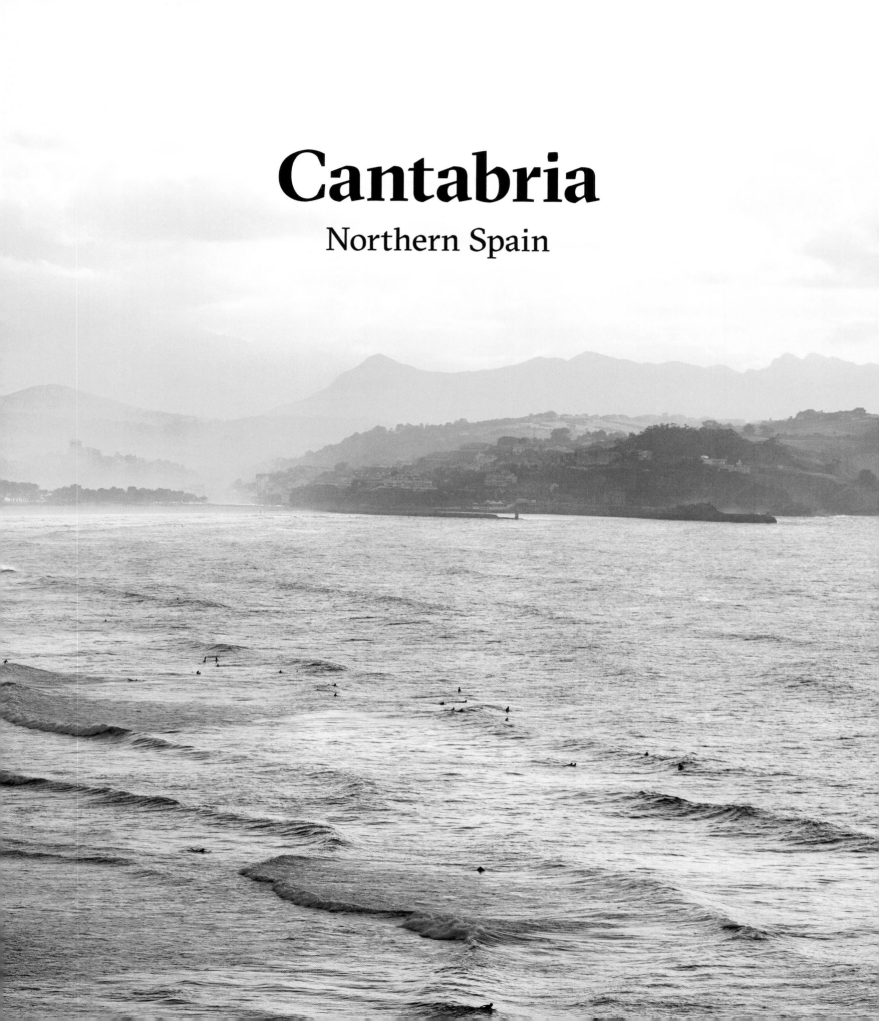

Cantabria

Northern Spain

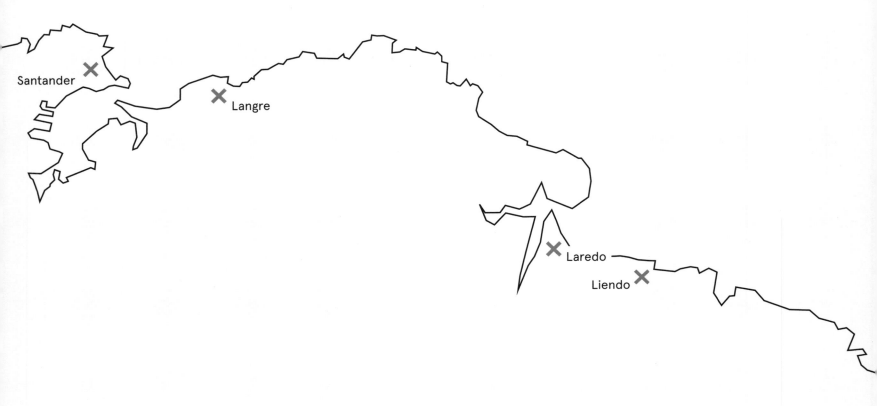

Santander

Langre

Laredo

Liendo

The area around Santander is considered one of the cradles of surfing in Spain.

The pioneers of the 1970s set out from the provincial metropolis with its 180,000 inhabitants to surf the surrounding natural jewels such as Langre, Liencres, Los Locos, or Comillas. The varied coastal landscape offers rocky cliffs and small hidden sandy bays, which, in addition to firstclass waves, also provide the necessary wind protection. The beaches face in different directions so that there is the right wave height for every swell direction.

At many spots we only meet surfers. Many come with their minibuses. Wetsuits hang over their doors to dry and ventilate, surfboards lie on their roofs, here and there we hear little snatches of music. Whether it's raining or the sun is shining, none of those who come out of the water dripping wet or those who are on their way in seem to notice. Some of them sleep in their vehicles parked in nearby meadows. While this is usually not allowed, it is tolerated. From Santander, we drive over winding roads along lush green meadows that almost reach the water – with the snow-covered mountain chain Picos de Europa always in the background. The

vastness gives us a feeling of freedom, which we later enjoy to the full while surfing. The unstable weather presents us with impressive panoramas.

We meander along the coastal road to the bay of Langre, one of the next popular surf spots on our map. The panorama here is more reminiscent of Great Britain than of Spain. A rugged rocky coastline with green cow pastures frames this small but beautiful bay. It fully faces north which allows relaxed surfing even with bigger north-west swells. In general anything works here, from western to north-western swells as well as winds from the south or south-west. A special highlight is the view from the parking lot. Anybody who travels with a van, stays there. In Langre we meet many surfers who feel very connected to the place and therefore keep coming back. Like Maria-Federica, who discovered surfing as a source of life energy during a sorrowful time. On the Atlantic Ocean of Cantabria she discovered the pure pleasure of being able to connect with nature, if only for a few seconds.

Cantabria, Northern Spain

Francois, Gaetan, Clarence, Thom

When I face a wave, I stop thinking about anything else. Each time is a thrill because every wave is different. You can ride 20 waves and not one is the same. You keep saying, just one more – and then it's another and another. We just stick around in the water until it gets dark.

"In summer waves are very rare near our home town of Montpellier. You get them in spring, late fall and winter. You might be able to surf once a week. Sometimes the sea is completely flat. You need wheels to be able to go and look for a better spot. That's why we've got the transporter, so we can go on holiday together and enjoy some perfect waves."

"It's a sport or an activity where your brain takes a backseat. You forget all your problems. Of course, it depends on your attitude, maybe you are trying to improve your technique, and very concentrated on what you're doing, but there's more to it than that; the moment when the wave lifts you up and you glide down it and feel it pushing you forward. It's so incredible."

Cantabria, Northern Spain

Maria-Federica

Everything that happens to
me on my board prepares me
for difficult times.

What can you do when you lack the power to face challenges? Maria-Federica of Treviso, Italy, went on a trip.

I OWE MY LIFE TO SURFING

It turned out to be the most important trip of her life, because she learnt to have confidence. A bit like the confidence of surfers, who can stay in the sea for hours, keep moving and take on the water. That wave is going to come sooner or later. Now she has that confidence. Maria-Federica didn't get it before. Now she does, "I owe my life to surfing."

Walking along the beach in Langre, Northern Spain, Maria-Federica has her board under one arm and in her other hand there's a baby carrier with her seven-month-old daughter in it. "My feelings can change as many times as the waves, but there's one that is especially strong, and it's akin to the way you feel as a mother, it's between you and the waves, it only lasts for seconds, but it's powerful. For a moment you feel in tune with them, totally connected. That's the moment!"

Maria-Federica used to work in the art world. It was hard and there came a point when she was totally exhausted. When her mother got seriously ill she felt so burnt out that she didn't know how to deal with things. The gleam in the young mother's eyes disappears, a shadow falls over her. "I was all over the place," she recalls, "I was in a self-discovery moment, and looking for an inner peace."

SURFING CAN SAVE YOUR LIFE

Santander was her salvation. Maria-Federica's bright smile comes back as she goes on, "This freedom that all surfers talk about, well I felt that with the first wave. Even as a beginner I got this powerful sensation of being connected to nature. When I was in the water I learnt to look truth in the face, to recognize it, to accept it and to draw vital energy from it."

Maria-Federica got in to surfing while she was studying on an Erasmus course. She was supposed to do it in England, but just before it began she made a trip to San Sebastian, and that's when it happened. She applied to have her Erasmus grant shifted to Spain. It worked. She went there instead, and spent 12 months going into the water every day. Since then – for the past 13 years – she's been coming back to surf at Langre just nearby.

Struggling with the waves, testing my limits, understanding who I am – that is the greatest feeling of all.

– Maria-Federica

Cantabria, Northern Spain

Cantabria, Northern Spain

Playa de Verdicio is a bay divided into two by a headland. It offers three different beaches and wonderful options for wild camping directly on the cliffs with sea views. On the low plateau with direct access to the beach we are almost alone and stay overnight. If you stand in the right place, you only need to lift your head in the morning and can see directly if the waves justify getting up early. In popular San Vicente it is also possible to camp on a sloping meadow with a view of the bay, but you have to pay a farmer for the privilege.

The two spots Playa Merón and Gerra have only little protection and tend to get too big quickly with big swell. Oyambre, a spot located only a few kilometers to the east - once uphill and once downhill - is more protected by a peninsula. This makes it the perfect alternative when Gerra and Merón are more scary than inviting for surfing. When you surf here, you don't really have to watch out for anything. There are no reefs or rocks. There is nothing but sand far and wide, which is why the spot is also very suitable for beginners.

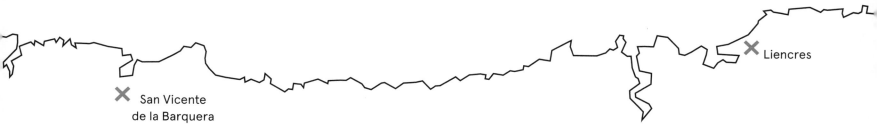

San Vicente
de la Barquera

Liencres

Cantabria, Northern Spain

Galicia

Northern Spain

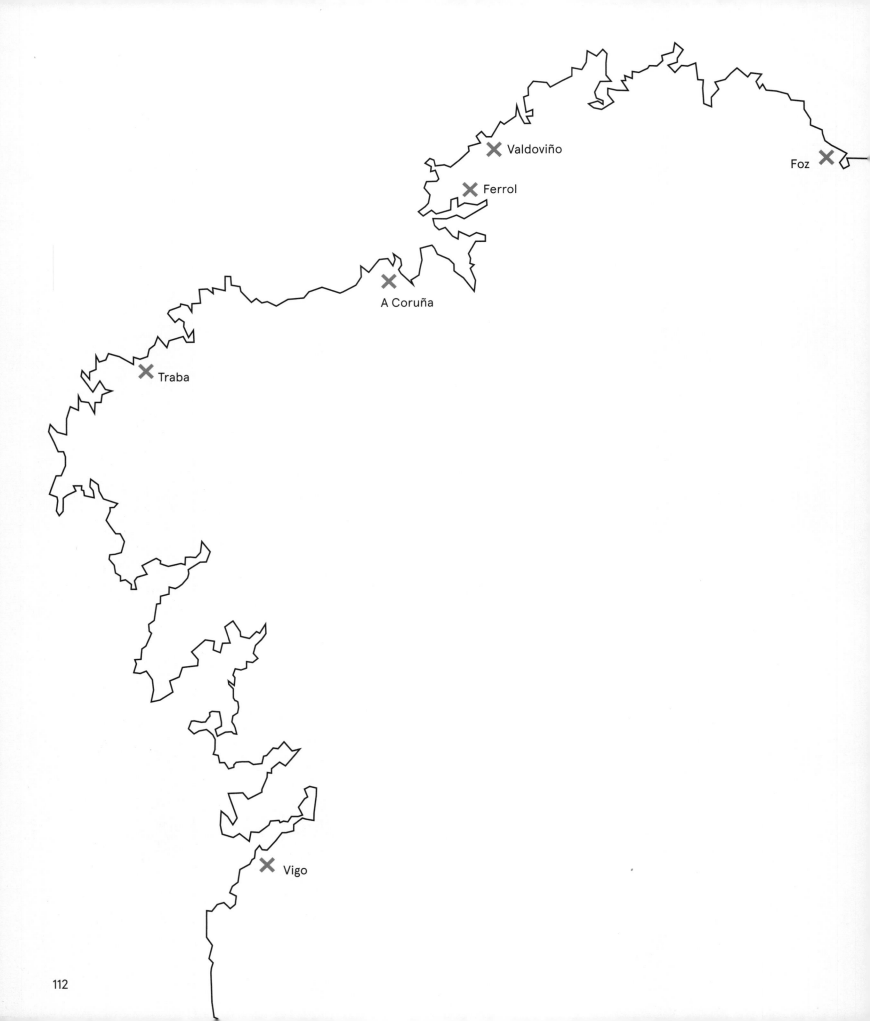

Valdoviño

Foz

Ferrol

A Coruña

Traba

Vigo

At the northwestern tip of Spain, the Atlantic Ocean shows its full force. Impressive big wave spots attract professional surfers and amateurs alike.

At the point where the Romans once assumed the world ended, there are strong currents and roaring winds. They push sets of waves in the direction of the coast, a breathtaking setting of cliffs and rocky shores, intercepted by solitary bays with golden beaches of various sizes, coupled with inviting coastal communities and fishing villages. The region is sparsely populated, a few kilometers into the heartland natural coastal forests grow, such as the Fragas do Eume – 9,000 hectares of luscious nature along a clear river.

In Ferrol we spend the nights all alone between the sky and the earth with the sound of the sea and a view of the waves. We feel at one with nature. Like everywhere else in Spain, the locals tolerate wild camping. Nothing could be better. It is one of the most beautiful moments of our journey. At the Doñinos beach the waves are perfect and friendly people gather for relaxed talks about the life of surfers, vans and waves. Head and heart continue to search for the flow in the water, but after demanding surf sessions, the muscles are exhausted.

Now halfway through our journey , we have to decide where we want to enjoy coffee from our Bialetti coffee machine the following morning, which lonely beach do we like best and which view will add spice to our dinner. After so much enjoyable wilderness we decide to visit the coastal town of A Coruña and enjoy some Galician tapas. Perhaps the Romans were right in some way. It is one of the ends of the world.

Galicia, Northern Spain

Daniel

Daniel is an engineer.
He's got his own bus for
when he wants to travel.

It's great to be in the water, on the waves. You can be in there for two hours or more, trying your luck, and at the end of the day, there might only be two or three times when you can say, that was just perfect.

PADDLING, TAKE OFF, AND RIDING THE WAVE

Daniel does a lot of sport, but he says being in the water the whole time is different from going jogging for example, because your're much more in touch with nature. There isn't a direct connection with his work, but every once in a while he gets "the great yearning", and "surfing isn't just one thing," he says, "it's a fascinating sequence of actions; paddling, the take-off, and then riding the wave."

THE CALM AND ENERGY OF THE SEA IS FASCINATING

He is a car lover who is often on the move, vintage cars, driving in rallies, roadtrips. When he goes home, it's the powerful memory of how he conquered this or that wave that lingers in his mind for a couple of weeks.

His biggest memory is from South Africa. He tried to surf a barrel and missed it. He crashed down, his board broke and the leash tore. Other than that, it is "simply beautiful" to lie on the water and experience the sunset, Daniel says enthusiastically.

Galicia, Northern Spain

Fred

We travel to surf, that's all we think about and dream about. That's why we're here. If it's not there, there's just something missing.

OUT THERE NOTHING ELSE MATTERS

Skipper Fred, from Argentina, works for a sailboat charter company in the Algarve, Portugal. "Water is my life," he says. "I was born by a big river where it flows into the sea in a sparsely populated area." This is why he feels a deep connection to water. As a child he spent a lot of time swimming, kayaking, and windsurfing. When he later moved with his family to the sea, he learned surfing and never stopped. Today he travels around with his camper and surfs as much as he can because he just likes the idea that out there, "nothing else matters".

THE SPORT REQUIRES CONCENTRATION AND BODY CONTROL

"Your only thought is to keep your balance and avoid falling, and to try and glide, keep a path open and come out the other end." This is how Fred describes the moment of happiness. "You haven't got any time to think," he adds. "In the few seconds you have on the wave, you're not paying attention to usual things. Your senses are tuned to external stimuli, like the texture of the water, is it choppy or is it glassy? You just feel the water. It's something else!"

IT'S A PASSION THAT AFFECTS ALL ASPECTS OF LIFE

Fred's constant search for the flow is like seeking the elixir of life. It keeps him on the road in search of it. As a boat skipper he comes up close to big waves, sometimes very big, but they don't compare with what he experiences when surfing.

There is nothing that matters to me except being on the water. I forget everything else around me.

– Fred

Northern &
Central Portugal

Portugal

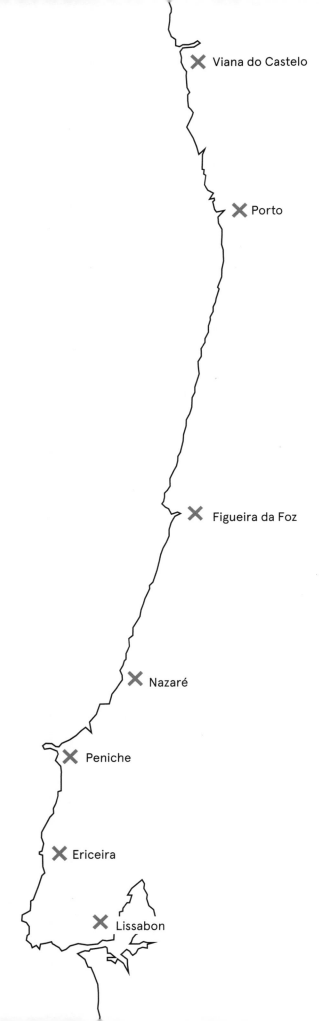

Viana do Castelo

Porto

Figueira da Foz

Nazaré

Peniche

Ericeira

Lissabon

South of the Spanish border, the Costa Verde extends between the estuaries of the river Minho in the far north of Portugal and the river Douro near Porto.

Extensive beaches and sand banks are situated in front of massive cliffs and white dunes. The bordering mountain regions with natural pine forests and hilly vineyards are sparsely populated. At the same time, dispersing swell rolls towards the beach and creates even set waves. When we are not blown away by the wind, we unfold the table and enjoy the sunset that is reflected in the water and on the cliffs, not a rare sight in the many secluded areas with a sea view where we stop to rest.

On the beach of Afife near Viana do Castelo, a sheltered cove, we wake up and it's foggy for the first time on our journey. On seeing this we decide to take a break for three days in a hotel. Next day we hit the waves in the early morning mist, the line up is empty. But after days of unstable weather with wind and random waves also affecting other spots like Praia do Esmoriz, the rain comes in and we are engulfed in a dark gray cloud. To escape we drive on south over mostly bumpy roads.

After a romantic night spent in Leiria, where the weather is sunny again, we reach Peniche. In and around the famous surf spot we meet people to whom surfing is everything – the Belgian Matisse, who lives here with his family to practice every day for his career as a professional surfer, and Jonathan from Israel, who is filled with such a great love for what he does that he meets everything in life with a smile. At the world-famous spot "Supertubos", crazily high waves break only a few meters from the beach. The Atlantic foams. In Ericeira the waves are also very big, massive wipe outs have become part of our surfer experience when we visit the next idyllic fishing township. After so many impressive encounters with the force of the ocean we decide to set up relaxed camp at a lovely location above the cliffs. We have now completed two-thirds of the road trip. The sea calms down somewhat towards the evening and we end the day with a campfire.

Matisse

Studying, getting a job – what "normal people" do, was never an option for Matisse.

MATISSE WANTS TO BECOME A PROFESSIONAL SURFER

When he's on his board he's got the freedom to do anything he wants. After only a couple of years he became champion of Belgium. "As soon as you win something, you get noticed, and you get approached by sponsors." It's only a few years ago since he first went out on a longboard in Belgium with some friends, "and Belgium has very small waves." Despite the sponsorship, surfing doesn't yet provide a living for the young champion, but at least his costs, like travel, equipment and food are covered.

THE WAVES RULE HIS LIFE

At the age of 16 he opted for home schooling to allow him to get on his surfboard every day. "That is all that I do. I dedicate my life to it." Surfing didn't just affect his own life, but that of his entire family. Matisse moved to Portugal with his mother and brother and now he trains every day. His father still lives and works in Belgium, but he comes to visit from time to time.

THE DECISION TO MOVE TO PORTUGAL HAS GIVEN HIM A GREATER SENSE OF FREEDOM

Despite his talent, the promise of success and the possibility of getting to know some stunning places, Matisse feels more at home when he's spending time surfing with friends. "Perfect waves, all day long with people you're close to."

The sea never judges you. There is simply no wrong or right when you are surfing a wave.

– Matisse

Jonathan

It has the greatest possible influence on my life. Each day I am motivated anew.

When you are standing on a wave, your head is empty, just like meditation, you are no longer connected to reality, instead you are connected to another world and in a dream. It's a feeling that you want to return to again and again.

– Jonathan

The adrenaline, the action and connection to the wave, this power cannot be put in words.

JONATHAN HAILS FROM A VILLAGE NEAR TEL AVIV

The 21-year-old is traveling around and wants to visit Australia soon. He loves snowboarding, surfing, and sailing. Three months ago he was still serving as a soldier for the military. He explains, "That doesn't mean I am a great fan of the system, but in Israel you don't have a choice, you have to do your bit." He was in the special forces that gave him the possibility of serving a part of his time onboard ship. It was difficult for him to have the sea so close and not be able to jump in. "I saw these great waves but I couldn't go in. That was the hardest thing, much worse than anything else."

IT WAS HIS TURN

In Hossegor, France, one day there was a really big swell. Only a few locals and Jonathan dared to go into the water. "I was really given a good shaking because the waves were so big," he reminisces, and as he lowers his voice and you can feel the respect in it. He goes on, "I was waiting for my turn." All the locals had already ridden their waves when a set arrived and it was time for me, everybody was shouting, "go, Jonathan go!" His voice becomes more excited as he recalls what happened, "I flew up into air, approximately three meters high, straight into the sky, then flew down again and was washed away. I managed to get out of that, but it was such a shock." Jonathan laughs.

SURFING IS THE LOVE OF HIS LIFE

"Let me put it this way: My girlfriend still does not understand after many years why I get up this early in the winter to go surfing. Well it would be hard not to. I'm addicted to it." Jonathan knows how much space surfing takes up in his life. Jonathan's heart is so full of the passion for surfing that his whole attitude to life benefits from it. "The energy and the vibe is so good, and it makes me feel so happy that I'm able to approach everything else in life more calmly and always with a smile."

Algarve
Southern Portugal

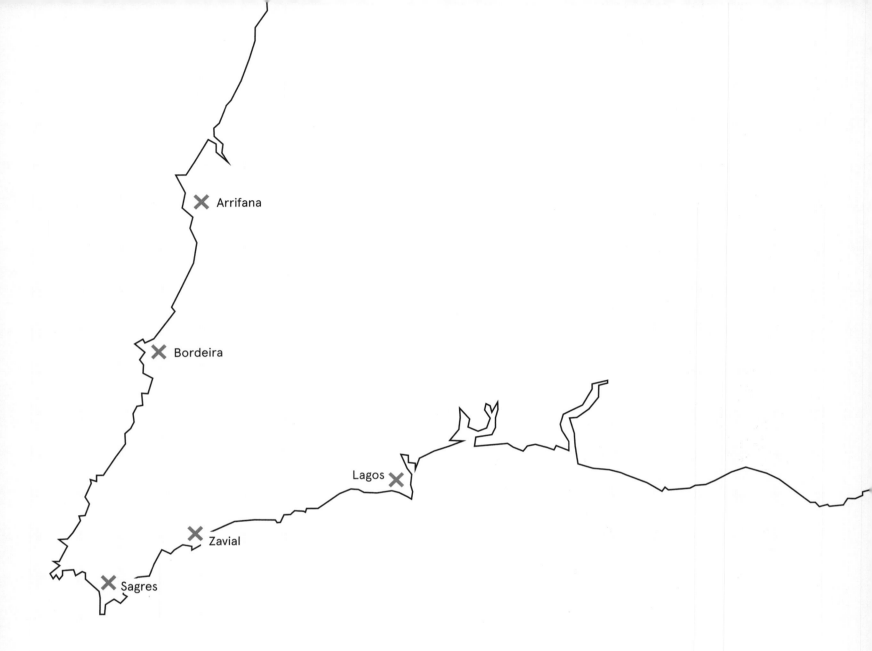

Arrifana

Bordeira

Lagos

Zavial

Sagres

In late fall following stops in Fonte de Telha, Lisbon, and Odeceixe we reach the Algarve. A thin light-gray mist dims the bright colors of the dream destination of surfers.

At first we can't see the horizon at Europe's most south-westerly tip but as the sky quickly clears up a bit further north on the west coast, the sun warms us up. The glistening light reveals the contrasts between the turquoise to violet-blue sea, the ochre-colored cliffs, and white beaches. The waves of the Atlantic have created cragged formations on the 200-kilometer shore line, 50 to the west and 150 to the south. Through a dune landscape covered in grasses and bushes, hidden tracks and paths lead to the most spectacular spots. Along the bendy roads, fully equipped vanlifers from all corners of the world are out and about. The water is dotted with small black specks – surfers waiting for the next ride. In this Garden of Eden for surfers you continuously see one or another rise up and glide for what seems an eternity along a wave.

Algarve, Southern Portugal

Algarve, Southern Portugal

Algarve, Southern Portugal

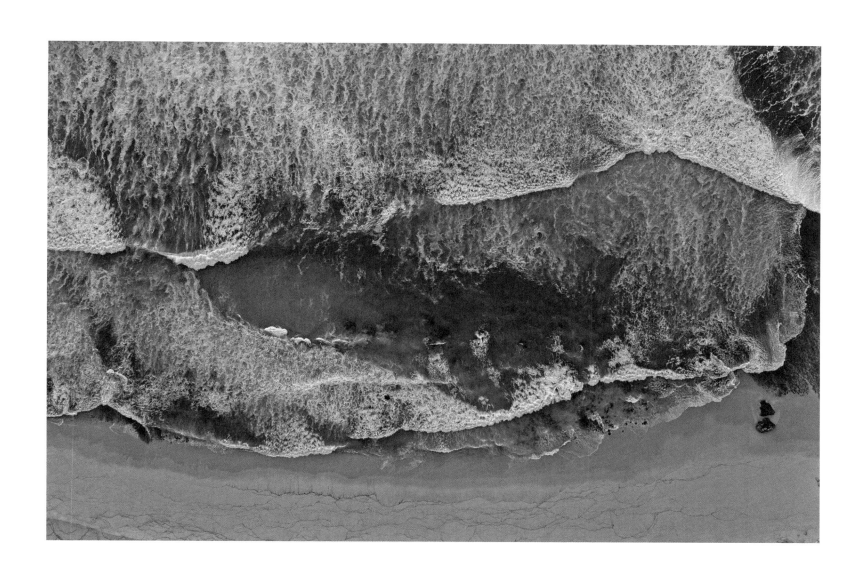

Algarve, Southern Portugal

Jesko

When I'm surfing I feel in touch with myself and my surroundings.

ESCAPING THE EVERYDAY LIFE

"Surfing gives you a very special opportunity to escape your everyday life and get into a different place." This gives the teacher from Hamburg a sense of security. "When something goes wrong in my life, I head for the seaside." As well as having this escape route out of bad situations, surfing has given Jesko self-confidence. "If I'm facing a challenge and starting to doubt myself, I often ask myself, how many waves have you conquered? How many years have you spent to get to this level? If you've had the tenacity to prevail there, and overcome the setbacks, you can do that in other areas of your life as well."

This kind of experience helps Jesko in his work. He teaches 14 and 15-year-olds at a special school in the Wilhelmsburg area of Hamburg. Jesko elaborates further, "There is social deprivation and the students have multiple problems. Some of them fear they will be forced to spend their whole lives in that area of the city. They think they will never escape," explains Jesko. "Even the geography does not help. Wilhelmsburg is like an island."

TRANQUILITY IN THE SENSE THAT I STOP THINKING OF ANYTHING BUT ONLY LIVE THE MOMENT

Exercising at the gym, swimming, bicycling, triathlon, yoga and climbing help him unwind from his stressful job. Jesko especially appreciates the serenity of surfing. He feels that time, space and his actions are one and he simply exists. "That sounds so pathetic, but this is precisely it, being in the here and now." Even so, excitement is also part of it, and Jesko knows all about adrenaline rushes.

There is always a bit of fear, but an activating type of fear.

– Jesko

Algarve, Southern Portugal

Andrea

When you ride a wave for the first time it is such a unique feeling that you can't find anywhere else.

When I am near the sea and can travel around with my bus – that is the definition of freedom for me. Simply moving on from beach to beach.

MAKE THE RIGHT DECISION

When you're surfing you face situations that can have an echo in daily life. It is actually all about mustering up the courage to do something. While the mental challenge is the same for everyone, she explains that there are different types of surfers. There are those who will go for anything, who have no second thoughts, and there are others who are a little scared. Andrea belongs to the more cautious group. To her it is extremely important to check out the conditions. "Surfing is similar to meditation. It allows you not to be constantly pre-occupied by your own thoughts. You can really switch off your mind and truly enjoy what you have at the moment."

ONE THING LED TO ANOTHER

Initially, Andrea was not very interested in surfing and had to be convinced to try it. Today she describes herself as a water lover. She found her passion surfing, on a trip to Morocco. So one thing led to another. Soon she became a surf instructor, like her boyfriend at the time, and they opened two surf camps in Galicia and Morocco.

Algarve, Southern Portugal

Our favorite spot is the Praia do Amado beach, which in the last few decades has become an El Dorado for surfers, yet it remains authentically wild and sufficiently expansive. Resembling long fingers, rock walls extend into the ocean to the left and right of the cove. There are hiking tracks near the water. Low tides push a uniform swell and create barrels. In some places the waves are too high, but the strong wind tantalizes us and we enjoy some full power windsurf sessions. At the multifaceted surf spots around Sagres the swell is also very strong. The breakers push foamy white against the rough, orange-colored cliffs, as if the sea was nibbling on them. During this season, on a single day there may be hardly a wave visible in the morning and then an incredible swell comes rumbling along. A big storm crosses our path and pushes the sea towards the land.

It is now colder in the mornings. In the far south of the Algarve the weather is pleasantly mild but the waves disappear. We return to Amado in search of the flow. We park our van here for a few days at a point from which we can directly see the beach and the waves.

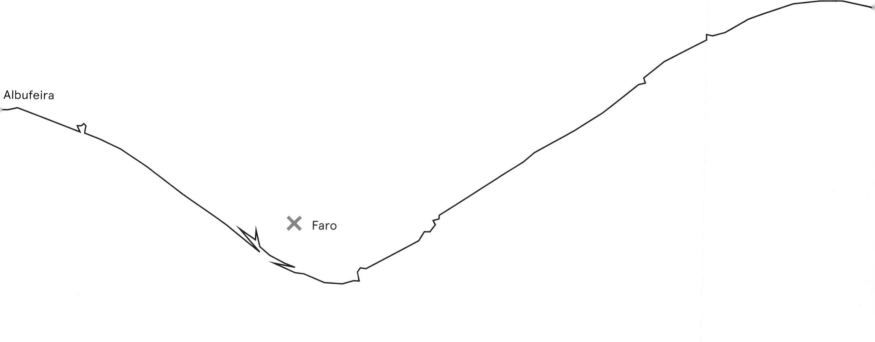

Albufeira

✕ Faro

Algarve, Southern Portugal

Andalucia

Southern Spain

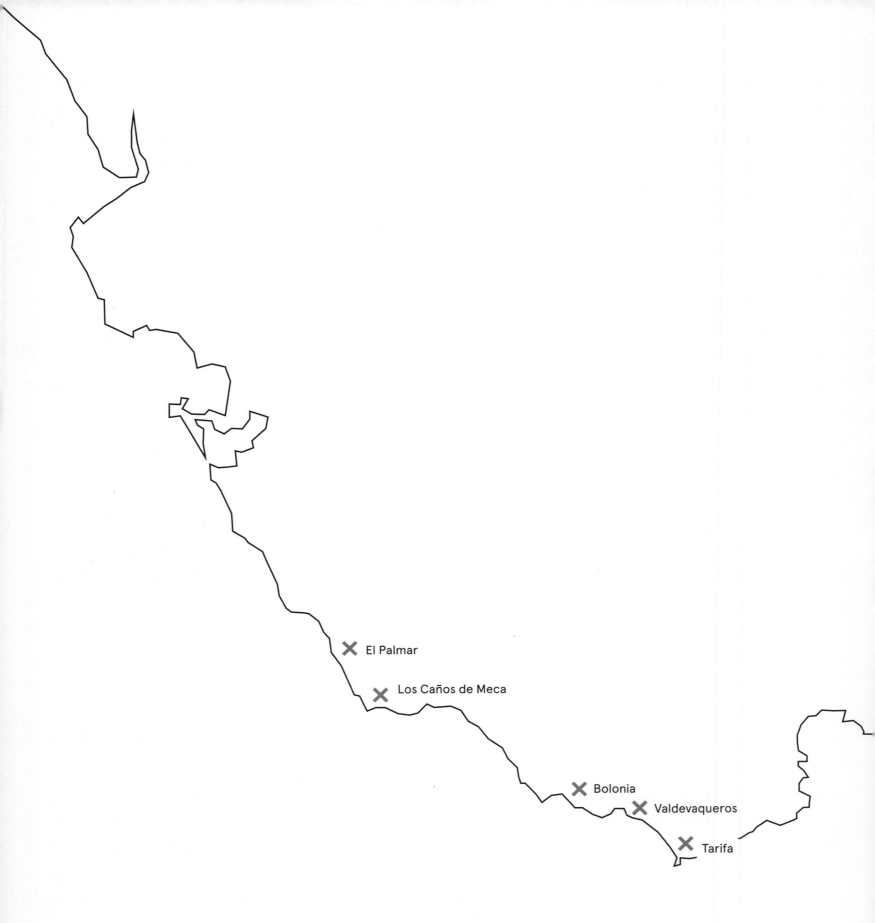

X El Palmar

X Los Caños de Meca

X Bolonia

X Valdevaqueros

X Tarifa

Just beyond the Spanish-Portuguese border we stop in Isla Cristina. The wind is tempting, the waves are breaking on the shore, time for some windsurf sessions. Then we head to one of Andalusia's most attractive spots, the swell magnet, El Palmar, 60 kilometers from Tarifa.

We park our van Alba next a few other campers and go for a swim in the orange light of the warm fall sunbeams. The Atlantic creates beautiful beach breaks over the sandbanks and the perfect conditions make it hard to leave the water. It is simply magical when everything is just right. The distances between the waves, their height, hardly anyone else in the line up, the warm sun that caresses your face and soul. This leads to the natural feeling that one is in touch with one's inner self, that one has come home.

Slowly we approach the end of the Atlantic coast. Tarifa, the "Wind Capital", the most southerly point of continental Europe is "vibrating". It's on the Straight of Gibraltar which is between 14 and 44 kilometers wide. Where Atlantic and Mediterranean meet there is a howling wind that lifts the fine sand of endless beaches and lets it dance around your body. Bright sunshine bathes Europe's southernmost tip in glittery light. Golden beaches extend for kilometers along the coast and compete with the bright blue of the water. The mountainous, rather rugged back country hides green oases and wonderful white mountain villages.

There is plenty of space for camping directly near the surf spot, even accommodating our hammock suspended between pines that are twisted from the strong wind. Morocco can be seen in the distance. From here it can be reached in only one hour by boat. Large container ships pass in front of the gray background, the north African mountain landscape. The big wide world seems so close.

Everywhere windsurfing sails scamper by, in between there are whitecaps like little brush strokes on the wave crests. Storms over the Atlantic create ideal waves in this section of the coast, which break particularly clean on the sandy ground of the Los Lances beach. In other areas, rocks under the water create good breaks, for example at the Hotel Hurricane spot. The beaches of Valdevaqueros and Bolonia extend desert-like to the mountain slopes. While the waves are often rather moderate, wind and kite surfers find perfect conditions on particularly windy days. With an inner feeling of peace and balance, in Andalusia we bid farewell to the Atlantic coast.

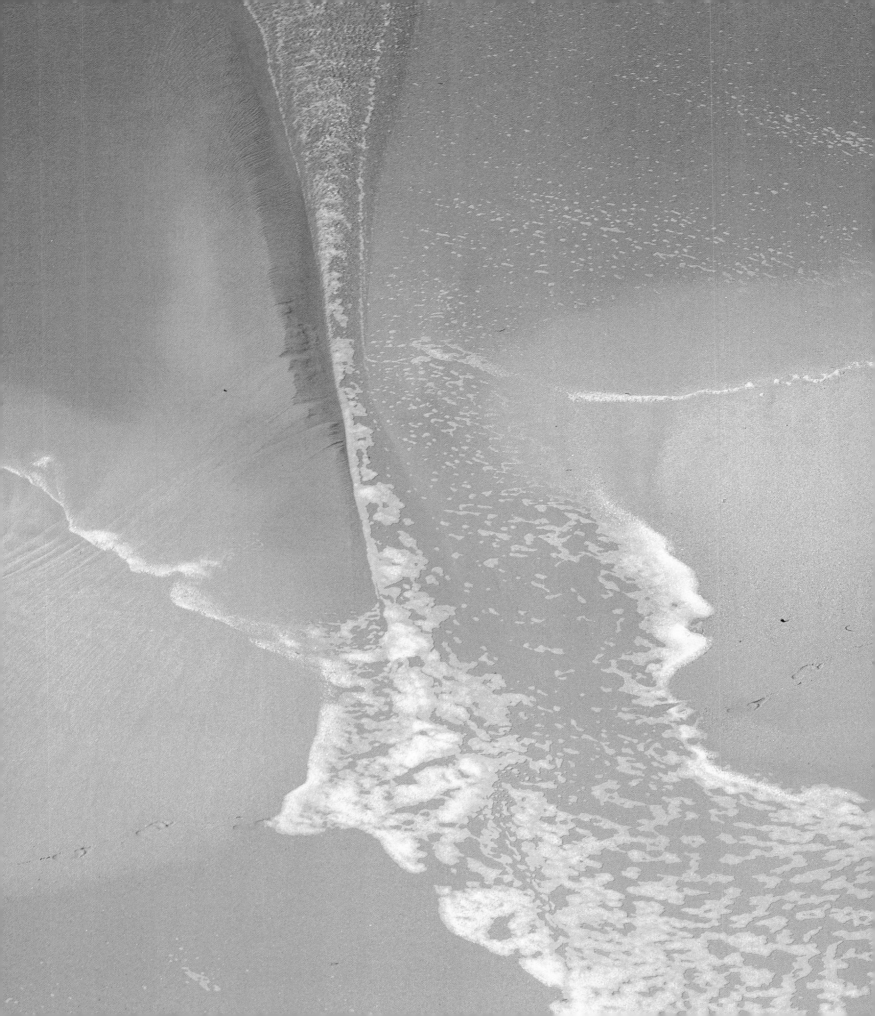

Fede & Tato

Fede lived in London and worked in various bars and restaurants, but then he opted for a nonconformist lifestyle and surfing.

He's actually been traveling for around 20 years. Fede has been surfing ever since his friends encouraged him to give it a try. Today he lives in an old converted rusty transporter, very simple and basic.

"When I ride a wave, the main thing I feel is freedom, as if mother earth was pushing me. It's a primeval force, brilliant but hard to describe."

My first thought after getting up is about surfing. That's why I check the forecast every morning. I do not mind driving many hours for good conditions because surfing means freedom to me.

– Tato

Andalucia, Southern Spain

Andalucia, Southern Spain

Andalucia, Southern Spain

Andalucia, Southern Spain

You can't
stop the waves,
but you can
learn to surf.

– Jon Kabat-Zinn

About us

BILIANA ROTH

Designer at a well-known advertising agency in
Zurich. Studied visual communications. She's always
been fascinated by nature – a fact that is reflected in
her work.

www.bilianaroth.ch

DOMINIK BAUR

Photographer for the last 10 years. Specialized in
portraits, reportage and advertising. His work is
characterized by attention to detail, a dollop of
patience, curiosity and the joy of meeting people.

www.dominikbaur.com

Imprint

CONCEPT, PHOTOGRAPHY AND LAYOUT

Dominik Baur, Biliana Roth

TEXTS

Sandra Ellegiers, Dominik Baur, Biliana Roth

TRANSLATION

Cosima Talhouni, William Moult

SPONSORS

Canon (Switzerland) AG
Canon Academy
Focuswater
Fotostudio Baur

SPECIAL THANKS TO

our friends and families,
all supporters,
the great people we met on our journey

The Deutsche Nationalbibliothek lists this publication in the Deutsche Nationalbibliografie; detailed bibliographic data are available on the Internet at http://dnb.dnb.de

© 2021 Benteli, imprint of Braun Publishing AG, Salenstein
www.benteli.ch

1st edition 2021

ISBN 978-3-7165-1860-1